Climates of the Mind

Climates of the Mind

Carolyn Mary Kleefeld

Introduction, and Collaboration in Editing,
Poetic Design and Organization
by Patricia Karahan

Foreword by Carl A. Faber, Ph.D.

Authors Choice Press
New York Lincoln Shanghai

Climates of the Mind

Authors Choice Press
an imprint of iUniverse, Inc.

iUniverse books may be ordered through booksellers or by contacting:

iUniverse
2021 Pine Lake Road, Suite 100
Lincoln, NE 68512
www.iuniverse.com
1-800-Authors (1-800-288-4677)

Printing History
1979 Limited First Edition, 500 copies printed by letterpress,
clothbound, reserved and signed by the Author.
1979 First printing, softbound
1980 Second printing, softbound
1981 Third printing, softbound
2005 Fourth printing, softbound

The original publication and the first three printings
of *Climates of the Mind* were by The Horse and Bird Press,
Los Angeles, California.

Library of Congress Catalog Card Number: 78-73648

ISBN-13: 978-0-595-36564-7
ISBN-10: 0-595-36564-7

Printed in the United States of America

Climates of the Mind

is dedicated to its godmother,

Patricia Karahan

and to its godfather,

Carl A. Faber

my most sacred and venerated comrades

Other Published Books by Carolyn Mary Kleefeld:

Kissing Darkness: Love Poems and Art, co-authored with David Wayne Dunn, RiverWood Books, Ashland, Oregon, 2001

The Alchemy of Possibility: Reinventing Your Personal Mythology, with a Foreword by Laura Huxley, Merrill-West Publishing, Carmel, California, 1998

Mavericks of the Mind: Conversations for the New Millennium, David Brown and Rebecca McClen Novick, Crossing Press, Freedom, California, 1993 (Includes an interview with Carolyn Mary Kleefeld, along with those of other leading-edge philosophers)

Songs of Ecstasy (Volumes I and II), Gallerie Illuminati, Los Angeles, California, 1990

Lovers in Evolution, The Horse and Bird Press, Los Angeles, California, 1983

Satan Sleeps with the Holy: Word Paintings, The Horse and Bird Press, Los Angeles, California, 1982

Soul Seeds: Revelations from the Mystery, to be published in 2006.

Since its original publication in 1979, *Climates of the Mind* has been translated into Braille by The Library of Congress. *"Climates," "Satan Sleeps with the Holy"* and *"Lovers in Evolution"* have been used worldwide as texts in university classes in creativity, psychology and human development. *The Alchemy of Possibility* has been used in university classes in art and psychology, and at healing centers.

To learn more about Carolyn Mary Kleefeld and her award-winning books and fine art, please visit her website at www.carolynmarykleefeld.com or call 800-403-3635.

Contents

Chapter of Visionaries   III

Chapter of Musings   IV

Chapter of Visages   V

Chapter of Spleen   VI

Foreword

This is an extraordinary book by an extraordinary woman. With great courage and innocence, she has vulnerably shown us the mystery of transformation. In a time of spiritual decadence, still another poet has injured us with the visions of possibility. Here is a rare wedding of poetry, philosophy, and psychological awareness, without the wooden self-consciousness of most modern psychological writing. Here are the timeless images of the unconscious erupting in a worthy vessel.

As with other invaluable books, there is a sense of the writer being carried, inspired, borne by great forces. Finally, this is a book of essence, the kind of book that informs and potentially heals its readers by communicating, with love, a sense of what underlies the particulars of their lives.

Carl A. Faber, Ph.D.
Venice, California
August, 1978

About the Author

Carolyn Mary Kleefeld was born in Catford, England and grew up in southern California where she studied art and psychology at UCLA. In 1980, she moved to her cliff-side home high above the Pacific Ocean in Big Sur, California, where she studies, writes, and paints amidst the wilderness around her.

With a passion for creative expression and a lifelong fascination with spiritual transformation, she is an award-winning poet and artist, whose books have been used as inspirational texts in universities worldwide, and translated into Braille by the Library of Congress. Her art has been featured in galleries and museums nationwide.

By Way of an Introduction....

As the Godmother of this book, I wrote this introduction, as a letter to Carolyn, to give you an understanding of the forces which have propelled her writings, and to explain the format of the book and the visual designs of the poetry.

Passion—as the sea, as the source of life—is the blood which is your soul, and your soul has birthed your poetry.

Your title reflects this force underlying your writing. Climates—sudden storms, earthquakes, droughts—ultimately spontaneous, propelled from a place beyond concept or definition; an alchemical source existing within the molecules of origination. You write of and from this source. You write outside of time.

You express your climates as thoughts, poems, poetic prose—but all poetry in its ultimate sense. Poetry as alchemy—a structuring, reshaping, collision of blood with experience; the gravitational pull of creativity.

You add to experience more than having experience add to you. Your poetry does not originate from learning. Rather, you bring what you are, the storms and seas within you, and from there, from that force, you absorb, totally become your experiences, and they become you. You blend your essence, the energies alchemize, and you write and emerge expanded from that alchemy. Your poems, "Hijacker," "Infused in the Infinite," "Survival Through Illumination," "Spiritual Bolero," and "Unnamed Source" express your living of this process with the elemental forces in the world.

Your Chapter of Visages and your poem "Primal Desire" express this psychic alchemy within your relationships. You write of actual people you know and have known, but more than that, because you blend at the level of blood and bring that out in others, you experience and write of forces and truths which go below obvious exteriors, and which comprise the very marrow of a person's existence. You see into their souls. You write of the dynamics of their passions and of your own, and of the forces which ignite them. You write of forces which underlie basic human motivations, encompassing more than the personal. You often ignite people to their own possibilities in this process.

Your inherent integrity refuses to compromise your spirit's total insistence on truth, meaning, value. But, you sense and see a surrounding world of hollow values. Having no external validation, you were wrenched temporarily from something primal—your sense of origin, your instinctual connection with basic spiritual truth—before you could know to value your beauty, uniqueness, your own intrinsic wisdom.

But, your driving instinct led you on a non-relenting spiritual odyssey, an odyssey to re-connect with origin. Your odyssey, and therefore much of your writing, is powered by your sense of disconnection underlaid by your inherent belief in a truth which transcends the spiritual destruction you see around you. You write from that sensing, at the level you feel it, below where you even consciously know, but where all your battles were fought. To seek such powerful truths, and to instinctually sense your connection with them, draws you magnetically to all you sense as powerful. You must alchemize with those forces—evil and death, as well as truth, beauty, love—in order to transcend them, in order to experience and know the dynamics of your own truths. You write of all these forces, with the power and the knowing of nature within you.

Your view of nature is Pantheistic. You feel nature as encompassing the universality of the truth you seek, and of which you write.

Because such truths seed metamorphosis, the Chapter of Metamorphosis follows. You write not only of a personal metamorphosis, but of a spiritual odyssey—an emergence through self-doubt, pain, destruction, to discover ultimately a oneness with the universe. This journey is expressed in the sequence of the poems in the Metamorphosis Chapter. The beginning poems, "Self-Doubt," "My Sister, the Moon," and "Seeking Self," are not your strongest poems, but are included to communicate all aspects of such a journey. They were written when you were just beginning, did not yet consciously know your inherent strength, and had lost your connection with origin.

Because you write of a spiritual odyssey, an odyssey through ultimate forces, the Chapter of Visionaries is closely intertwined with the Chapter of Metamorphosis. The Metamorphosis Chapter shows more of a process, whereas the Visionaries Chapter shows forces which underlie a true spiritual metamorphosis. By placing the Chapter of Visionaries after the Chapter of Metamorphosis, you show that through the process of metamorphosis, the truths of the dynamics in the Chapter of Visionaries can be sensed, discovered, and lived with awareness. However, the first three chapters flow naturally throughout each other.

Chapter of Musings expresses your whimsical, frolicking, inquisitive passion, a natural extension from the intense alchemy of your inner dynamics, and a necessary freedom in that constant alchemy.

Chapter of Spleen, your last chapter, expresses an eruption of your passion into anger, an anger moleculed in the power of the discoveries you have made, through your own metamorphosis, of your own truth, of innate truths which underlie what is universal, what is nature. This power of connection with origin, expressed in the last poems of your Chapter of Metamorphosis, alchemized your prior feelings of self-destruction, doubt, isolation, into anger at a world which has lost this connection, and which is stagnating in passivity and spiritual death. You can now sense your own being as transcending such static limitations. You see the world from your own reality rather than being victimized by what it is not. Your entire Chapter of Spleen expresses incredible strength, and should inspire people with extreme courage also to evolve beyond the world of concept, expectation, and definition, and to create and claim their own world.

The thoughts were written separately from the poems, but are arranged opposite poems which share in essential meaning.

Since all you do, you do with such intensity, you have done more than just "write" your poems. You have further infused them with individual identities through giving each a distinct form, placement on the page, arrangement of the title, punctuation, according to what the poem is communicating. People should experience rather than read this unique treatment, using their imagination to feel what you are saying. "Their Father—the Fisherman," "Unshared," "Hibernation," and "Electricities" are some examples of meaning integrated with and enhanced by visual design.

Your poetry is not grammatical. Rather, the power comes from the words themselves and the images they create. Because all is alchemical, mercurial, you use few periods. You use other punctuation, spacing, capitals, to communicate moods and to enable people to pause if something is particularly difficult to absorb, or to speed on if the tempo or the meaning demands it.

Also, your capitals often indicate when a new sentence or thought begins. You may have no capitals where they may otherwise be, such as "i", to show a loss of or weakened identity. Sometimes you use capitals and lower case letters to show domination of one power or person over another. The punctuation is totally organic, and to be "read" as integral with the poetry.

People can now experience all you have birthed, struggled, discovered, bled, felt at universal levels. Your five years of creating this book, and the centuries before that have been lived, are now alive, exposed, freed, birthed into the world. It is a most ultimate gift, an ultimate symbol of spiritual survival, a recognition and a validation of the power of primal truth. You have triumphed into the freedom of the infinite. And, you inspire those who will feel you at your essence, to explore such freedoms within themselves.

Patricia Karahan
Venice, California
August, 1978

I

Chapter of Pantheists

if it were not for nature, I would wonder more—
there seems more enemies in life
than
poets, heroes, warriors

Stepping out
    of her baptismal seas
        She began to seed her global gardens . . .

    Luxuriant pines stretch their spines tall and wide
    to house us from the beautiful beasts
    that feed and clothe our needs and more

    Endless wells of life's waters
    spring as raging arteries
    from the rich deep palms of earth
    Sparkling through our streams of veins

    Powerful soft arms
    outstretch to embrace and warm her kin
    Spreading her skirts out wide
    for opulent banquets of endless hospitalities

    Awakening us with tinkling bells
    of musical feathered clocks
    Cloaking our weary souls
    with cool silvery shrouds
    Bedding us down
    with the velvet pillows of darkness

    An infinite family
    lives in the pulse of her incessant tides

    Is it only in our dusts of death
    that we fertilize her womb of soil?
    For once unable to ask for a return

when we can not change or control something
there is a relief—peace in our awareness of its autonomy
as in the glory of nature

Life

I knelt, entranced, gazing into a transparent pond
Ocean splashed into being, bordered by bearded chins
        of jagged rocks
I felt, saw the totality, beauty of this self-contained
         miniature aquatic world
The miracle of its autonomous evolvement

Choruses of little fish glide in chords of musical notes
their scales the colors of sandy granules
Crabs languidly move under fitted speckled vests
        matching moss and rocks
Crawling, returning in freedom
A symphonic harmony of color, texture, function

The orchestration of this little world
       sings in one rhythmic breath
Heralding Life's untampered perfection

preceding gave thought to

       All lives have no being without Nature
       Nature's being Is without others

       Nature is the universal womb
       Totality   God
       All that lives, propagates within
       this self-generating circle of conception

the bee and the ant remain unchanged
in instinctual patterns of repetition—
static behaviors that for man effect decay

gave further thought to

> The quality of the need for survival
> designs the evolvement of all life
>
> This qualitative need
> is innate
> What is for one
> a suitable adaption
> for another is death
>
> These adaptions express themselves
> in unique form, color, texture
> > > > rhythm
> They exemplify
> the inborn uniqueness of expression
> necessitated by the need to survive
>
> This will to live
> The transcendental force
> is the ambulance sent by life
> to insure its infinity
>
> The quality of evolvement
> and availability of energy offered
> by a particular life form, determines
> what type and amount of life's dosage
> is receptive to assimilation
> how it is integrated—
> also, the timing of the cycles
> at which this survival dynamic travels
> > > > > to rescue

Trees

Limber spines sway to propelling rhythms
Emerald sprouts jewel tender boughs

Some grow to be confined
inhibited by rigid roots

Others form tiresome bushes
rounded in monotony

Transforming ones evolve with the seasons
unafraid of change

Parental limbs embrace
bending low to share rich fruits

Blossoms medal winning flowers
breathing smiles of sweetened scent

Weeping willows surrender
fertilizing graves for new sons' births

Tearing winds leave
barren leafless victims

The hollow tree trunk
echoes life's vacancy

Milk from the Skies

nocturnal dew
nourishes life
silently enveloping
with nurturing softness

the night's honey
soothes thirsty souls
with balms of renewal

the celestial queen
reigns independently
observing her spurry stars
                shimmer
upon bucking waves

constant father-sea
          promises
eternal fertility

night gives
universal birth
     in its
placenta of restoration

The Moon is a Memorial

the moon was once a sun
   whose rays ignited heat

radiance transformed—

nocturnal beams illuminate,
   transcending her remoteness

transfusing breath into past spirits,
   moving their misty shadows
     amongst the living

an effulgent memorial—
   reverent to what is
        has been

Oh the poem of what I feel
 leaps out of me—
  into herds of bounding deer
   upon dappled leaves
    that fly the winds
     lifting me into the lightest air
      breathing thousands of wings into my being

Oh the poem of what I feel
 flutters me into coral blossoming parasols
  Their reddened wet lips
   bend from strong stems
    facing gleaming grasses
     inviting me to dry
      from warm rains

Green accordion hands
 of many fingered ferns
  grace my shoulders
   I am stilled by their wondrous perfection

Cone-shaped castles
 of white frills
  dangle with the heaviness of soaked laces
   They appear frosted
    in this tropical storm
     shimmering in drenched happiness

        I, my child
         fly above wet cinnamon earth
          covered in island leaves, nuts, slushy fruits
          We're drawn into the sky's showers
           raised by a rainbow of velvety butterflies
           held by colors so deep, so vibrant
            Their perfumes incense us above ourselves

         This baptism everywhere bathes a new-ness, fresh-ness

         Our music sings in the mystic exaltation
          of living the poem of ourselves

         Nature lives within us for these moments

Rainwalk on Stinson Beach

Undiffused sea-beach energies
           balloon my lungs with delight
Frisky currents of maverick air
           lift me above the sands
My spirit soars
           as a kite without a tail
I wait to join
           the seagulls in flight

      Momentarily
      anchored
      by
    tears flooding my throat
I am pained by the ebullient joy
      of
claiming ecstacy as part of my being

I am reverent to this transcendental force

The skies lightening
           ignites my electricities
I prance
      cohesed in the eternal dance
Insistent needle points of rain
           pinprick my face
The aqua-puncture of elation

I, soggy clothed, wet-lashed
    foggy as the day
        bathed in moody muted algae shades
          colors of nature's beginning eyes
            are the water colors
             of my being
                Blending with embrace
                 liquefying me
                    into the purifying rain

Night

Trees
    stilled in wisdom
        breathe secrets of centuries
           in mystic silence
                through their silhouettes
                    laced intricately
                        against the falling sky

Between darkened branches,
    stars shimmer—
        mercurial leaves
           free'd
                to soar the night sky
                transcendent

Spellbound,
    I feed myself
        from wells of root
           So fed—
                I'm carried
                    upward, outward—
                      becoming endless
                        in the nocturnal mist

lying here on the softest earth
the rain just falls upon my face
the sounds of its full streams nearby
    fill me with their pulse
this milk from the gifting skies
    velvets me, my soul
washing away weariness of old tears
a cleansing for love's joys

Opaque Mirror

The moon's sullen self
                    just stares
Blocking my reflection

Rejecting answers
              a past
                    or tomorrows

Demanding existentialism
                    in her expressionless meaning
The changes in her shape
                  inspire trust

The sky is an ocean, a lake
  Cloud waves roll
    their billowy foam
      scalloping airy shores—cliffs

At the silhouette of day
  they move as smoky darkened islands
    sometimes merging
      fogged in by feathered spray

Tides, currents conduct
  compose with invisible batons
    electrical symphonies and boleros

Sometimes a lullaby
  on a soft day
    rocks the sea-sky's face

a universal truth
is a totality about any aspect of reality

Forget Technology

I'm looking through
my sun-warmed hair
        into a
meadowed few inches of life

It is all there

Within the wheat's waving golds
Every stem that breathes

Is all there is

Death Births Life

Nature has insistent pride
No shame in death

A proud trunk appears stilled
  but then reveals
    joyous sprouting
      of fresh emerald births

Fire

the air is unavailable—still—toxic
when nature is forced to surrender
science fiction becomes
the nightmare of reality

skeletons of ash float
hysterical flames scream
into innocent skies
where the sun lies
smothered by tyrannical atmosphere
dazed by its involuntary loss of projection—

an ill thing
impotently casting
its ghoulish sick light
the eerie heat born from disaster

the fire's wounds weep
blood upon the sea

an eyeless night follows
hiding from the horror
allowing suppression for rest
in its healing womb of darkness

the sea is quiet
bearing the earth's agonies
soundlessly below the waves

Revelation

Wildflowers verse with symphonic breezes
    portrait faces of random colors
       compose stemmed networks
        of insistent voices
          calling up to me

We answer your complex questions of life
    how do we start   why must we end
      there is no life   death
        just different expressions of each other
       wedded to one another
        in mutual sustenance

The eternal breathes
  within our blossom

Look—
  We need not be planted   To Be

  Our seed lives in the infinite

II

Chapter of Metamorphosis

I stomp down brush
to find the trees of my skeleton

we must live the unlived deaths of our parents
in blood first
before we can live our lives in choice

the world of myself
is the lamp that illuminates what I can see

you're in reverse gear with a tank full of gas

I murdered myself the other day
without mercy

Self-Doubt

Thrashing
Reaching
Tongue-ing Out
Grasping
Feeling
to Try to find out
What is the meaning of life I scream
Breathing
Eating
Waking
has been
an endless dull maintenance
to stay alive
Alive?
in what way
i pray
my heart beats
yet
sinks in decay
Decay from What
no love?
is that what's abey?

or is this body an empty thing
needing to feed
on others to bring
life to itself
since it's really dead
unable
to love?
felt   but
unsaid

Vacancy

i have
window eyes with vacancy signs
mere mists of me drift
behind my curtains
no one is welcome
i'm not home
can others see there's no occupancy
until i find me
to return
behind the windows of my eyes

My Sister, the Moon

The moon
hung
so dreadfully heavy
in the midnight stillness

A faceless phantom
floating lifelessly
casting on currents
below
a silvery sad soul
with
ripples of unheard sighs
reflecting meaningless unshapen shadows

I was returning
to the city
far
below me
with its obscene mask
of facetious lights
no part of me was there
not in one light
or
shadow

I was alone in the skies
with a heart
so
anchored
with
hurt
it left no space for me

Casting on currents
below
a silvery sad soul
with
ripples of unheard sighs
reflecting meaningless unshapen shadows

Seeking Self

Riding the crescent saddle
of the moon tonight
I feel her incompleteness
as part of me

My hesitant fingertips
seek to touch
the silver spurs
of
those swirling worlds
My curiosity ignited by
the entity behind its glow

I am overshadowed
by
the untamed space of timelessness

The moon cycles to fulfill herself
when she rounds out her face
A wombular self of infinite creativities
I feel when my arms enclose me
circular like her
for that moment
I am an entity of my own

I remember when my spirit embraced another
in a birth of our own completeness
that transcended all atmospheres
was beyond the light of knowing
Our union was a summer of wholeness
a shared spring of fertility
nurturing our souls

As the moon wanes I pale
Still reaching to touch
the elusive shores of those unknown worlds
Their eyes masked by
my unanswered questions

The moon's face begins a new life
My essence cycles on
                with hers

Clarification

The turbulent oceans of my mind erupt
   demanding entrance through closed doors

A noble need   now freed surges
   to clarify these currents

Interim caves of isolation
   contain reservoirs of energy necessary
                        for new freedoms
                              and

                  to stand breathing above
                  the draining undertow

heredity is the soil
our parents plant us in
until our roots become feet

we need to die the deaths of our parents
because they never lived them

one must transplant
when dwarfed and cramped as a potted plant
your roots have outgrown their soil

life is a promise—
a circle of beginnings
giving birth to beginnings
that expand wider and wider
enwombing a larger and larger world

Beginning

Thrashing down the brush of heredity
   society and all "ities"
I clear paths defining my chosen life
I envision my world
My paths are virginal, unmarked, unlived

My fright is balanced by an expectant hope
Hope that my relentless instincts
   have not misguided me
That my virginal claimed land
   is where my being can breathe its fullest self

I dread the isolation I feel is part of it
I need to share it as I live it
I know I will walk with hesitation
   until I can fully live myself—with confidence

My need to be there
   is stronger than I
I am at my own mercy

I have lived half my life and
   am only beginning
Thinking about it makes it difficult
   to find enough air to breathe

I hope my children's paths will be less muddy
   their energies not so spent
     clearing away dead confusing brush
But rather in walking forward
        with confidence
     toward their choices of self-defined births

interesting how each plant or person
has its own unique rhythm, cycle, form—
as long as it becomes the bloom of itself
its music of evolvement matters not

the sky is a gigantic stomach
all inside on earth are its births
some need to get out of this world first—
to enable birth

Death

extinguished,
she folded
her gildless
butterfly wings

clamped in a self-made trap
needle mouthed scars
had pinned, snagged
her fragile rainbowed sails
staining them a blackening red

her velvet center was shorn
too tangled in conflict
to ascend

Evolvement

I wait quiescently
   in the gossamer of cocoon

Naked eyes avoid raping light
  Metamorphosis parents green flight

My paradisical expansion
  spirals soundlessly
     into the nocturnal waltz
        of time and space

This propulsion in its exultation
      lifts   spreads
     my inpenetrably painted wings

The Costume of Evolvement Is . . .

i'm in mourning
        for my missing self
                i was so much fun
                        wasn't i

should i wear black
        who will be coming back
                what should i wear

i'm not yet the person
        i'm becoming
                maybe gray is more appropriate

    actually i don't like either color

I feel I am entitled
to choose the environment of my mind
not allow it to become a city dump for other people's trash

Prelude

I want to do, be, eat, sleep, hear
   without exterior reactions to my being
I want to be an invisible being—
   not defined, judged, watched

I do not want to represent anything to anybody
   no longer to be inside
   the other person's rigid picture frame of me
I want to be—just for the sense of being
To relax again enough to taste, touch, realize life
   before it is filtered through to me—
   through other people's psychic strainers
   through their telescopic needs
I want it fresh for me to grasp
   before it's had so many hands on it first
Just mine to embrace, discover, share
   or not share
A privacy, intimacy of me to me—
   whatever this may be
   to relate directly from where it lies

I breathe a deep breath
   at the thought of new discovery—
An intimate first-hand glide with life in my hand
   with me connected directly
No filters, no microphones
No need for closed doors; instead—
Open windows   Wide skies
No hands on life's clock
Another chance to feel that part of me
   that is undiluted
My life to belong to me
   to consistently feel its essence

Where My Book Was Born

This house is my home of harvest
A harvesting of my interior trees
Patient trees that now are rooted within me
at last blossoming the fruits of my core

I lean towards the electrical hair of the sun's beams
They transmute growth, color, a rounding
My essence is released to flow from its unlimited source
undammed by the compulsive mechanical spasms
                                                    of reaction

I let the antennae of my senses
inhale deeply—exhale without hesitation
No need for the armor of defense

I'm off the wheel of repetition
No longer treading its flatness

I have carpeted this house with the threads of my integration
I sit on this carpet in the chrysalis of my flower
My leaves open
glistening with meaning
My life-power unfurls,
its perfume enveloping me in the eroticism of its exultation

I am a flower opening to itself—within itself
My interior cradle of being is rocked, soothed
in this mellifluous balm of evolvement

(continued)

This is an anonymous house
one with no ego or pride
Unpossessive in its lack of demands
Healing in the catharsis of no past
No over-stuffed drawers of yesterdays
competing with todays
This wooden womb is painted a peeling grey
so right for its neutral passivity

A tree house perched high off the beach—beyond gaze
I'm seen only by the celestial sentinels
so sublimely suspended in space
I touch these distant worlds in feeling
reaching higher and higher
until my finger tips are patined
in the silver of their mercury

I return for rest
to nestle into
peer from my nest in the sky
High up as if in a jungle
to sense the rhythms
breathe with their tides
feel the pulse of the elements
be more in touch with my own heart beat

This house is a manger
Its honesty is sacred—
the innocence found in birth
No other place have I been born—so many times,
added so much life to my life

(continued)

There's a symphonic coalescence
between the pulse of my streams
and the seas outside
My dynamics claim the freedom
the abandon born of the gypsy winds

The untamed gardens of the sea
offer me a palatial everchanging playground
The tides landscape these nomadic gardens endlessly

The plasma of the sea gives without loss
Gifting me with waterfalls
that cascade inside me into ideas—
pools of imagination to swim in

(*continued*)

Strata of myself settle upon each other
until there is a mountain of me
I find less and less struggle against fragmentation

I am still a blotter, sponge
absorbing my environments, people
Experiences filter through
Some take a powerful hold of me
like the symbols of a Rorschach test
Others flit—
no identifications of impact are made

But, the Rorschach symbols
these mythological fiends of life—death
these birthmarks below the last layer of skin
under my mountain of self
They stay
their footprints self-cast in blood
Tattoos, remaining untouched by the wash of waves
these are the pains, ecstacies that meet me
challenges that provoke, inspire

All this possible in my manger of harvest

living death's birth
lets my passions, experiences, claims go—die
freeing myself of their limiting heartbeat
allows a space to reappear within me
I can feel—sense the birth of another pulse

The Labor Pains of Creativity

I'm like a hive of eggs walking around
    bumpy with pregnancies

My experiences collect the honey
    My ideas are hatched
      by the heat of imagination
        incubated in passion

My eggs are in various stages of growth
    ready for different times of birth

Some are twins
    not identical, but opposites
      called Con-flict
        neither one will allow birth

    Then there are
      my identical twins
        named Con-form
    Each conning their form
      to remain form-less
    Refusing earthly life
      swallowing me
    Bearing me down
      with their symbiotic dependencies

Having the labor pains
    but not delivering

Realizing only I can liberate myself
    from the greedy needs
      of them, me

So pregnant with myself
    with the bustling voices
      of my hive

Wanting to give birth
    Cut the cord
      Break the shells

      Panicked
that my hive is larger than i
        Aware
I must wing my powers
          Must deliver
or—be poisoned by my own unborn

Hijacker

I am the hijacker of my own missile
   carrying in-board
     my own personal explosion

          When life's electricities
         overcharge my fuses
       they blast me
      further than I am

My molecules afire
   fall as
     dying clowns burning
       their eyes flickering
         fighting passionless darkness

         Fragmented
       they drift
      becoming
     anonymous sands

Exhausted
   I drag the beach of myself away
     I peer upon my trails
       to understand where I've been

(*continued*)

I then let the waters, green of life
    bathe me
        roll lusciously over me

                Until the currents
                    transmute their electricities
                into my sands

The tides encourage my sculpture to re-form
    and
        I rise above the flatness

                    Then, to capture the ecstacies—the pains
                I write words
                    that before
                were merely bovine herds
                of inanimate letters

Now, through my transfusion
    the words go red
        Pulse
            Live lives of their own

                Each time read
                    A new voyage traveled
                        down different veins

my soul is paralyzed with the thunder of its solitude
the walls of the universe echo my pain

Healing

I am draining
        purging pain from every pore
Spiked boots
        have punctured my pores . . .
       sprinklers left on
      to drip
          ooze
           spill
      in spite of themselves
       drown the grasses of my being

These weary waters
       form a lake
           larger than i

Now that this lake is outside of me
           I can see my reflection
              matching me
               with clarity

                I yell
                 My echo is intelligible

Transitions

Volcanic earthquakes split—plough
exposing expectant
fertile soil
a yawning sweetness rises

Skies sob torrential storms
purple fire
sets alight
vibrant green

Agony's rivers carry away the crust

the purest honesty requires spontaneity—
honesty, spontaneity, curiosity are all parents
essential to re-creating life—
courage is their platform to live from

I'm more alone
because there's more of myself to be alone with

Courage

I refused the circus
        now I walk my own tightrope
           outside the massive tent
My white arms flung wind-spread
          into spacelessness
No shouldering branch
      or supporting breeze
        for balance
Vertiginous amidst such vastness
       I spiral around and around
         unfurling into vacuous spheres
I grasp hollow air
     wavering in the currents
I reach the center of my rope
      stretched so high—so taut
        only blackness meets
          my fall

Then I stop, and remember
      performing inside that doomed tent
      jumping through hoops
       riding nude upon prancing ponies
Exulting
   from rows of eyes
     mirroring applause
       blinking, clapping
Reflecting their psychedelic creation of me
I had belonged to those
    who didn't
    couldn't know me
      and
I could not claim a self
   myself
    until
I walked my own tightrope
     realizing
       over there
         in that airless tent
         Performers are encapsulated
         dazed
         within stunting acts

the more defined I—my world becomes
the greater the necessity
to refine, sift out
what of other worlds enters

I am a porcupine at times
in order to keep what is within—inside

they look at us with the hate of themselves

No More Rip-Offs

I will not be there anymore
for the hangovers of abuse

I will not answer with myself
to those not truly there
the people who do not listen or care

Those insulated against life
are not alive

I am allergic to their plague of boredoms
It takes days to purge their poisons

My anger distorted
thwarted by
what they are Not

I value my life
its rediscovered gold, honey

     I will discriminate

I'd like to go away and leave myself at home

Rest Needed

my Eyes are lid-less
my Skin end-less
my Roots shaken
        I'm in flight without freedom
             OverRipe

       I want to live
           from
               in front of myself for awhile

I can not tolerate organized emotion
it kills
the spontaneity of discovery through the senses

Spiritual Bolero

I'm like the birds with moon-followed feathers
    nautical compasses
        navigating the course of nocturnal tides
      they don't fly away as I walk by
        they aren't afraid of my shadow
                    as I
Unlike them
    there's only one of me on the beach tonight
Unlike them
    I've been swallowed by the currents
      punched under waves
        landing on parched sands

    I can't follow the tides in groups
      only getting my feet wet
        able to fly off at will

    I dive into deeper places
      and get too wet
Unlike them
    and their unrehearsed rhythms
      My instincts separate me from the rest
        except here—there
Unlike them
      I question why
      Why my eyes feel punished, bruised
        from so many nonconnections—so short fused
Unlike them, tonight
    I tasted the tears of my own blissful rain
      born from the rapture of this sweetest of nights

    My soul thunders serenading its radiance

    My unfeathered arms reach out
      in ecstatic absorption of this life

    The sea-night sky of shoreless worlds
          becomes me   mine
    The moon absorbs my essence
      and so rounds herself
            ahead of her cycle

Infused in the Infinite

In this uterine opalescent world
 of sky monotoning sea
  I breathe, move in cadence
   with the cosmic pulse, tides

The froth of effervescence
 giggles between my toes
  laughing into my being

Muddy sands mold evanescent shoes
 that instantaneously glove my feet
  Stepped out of
   they are left dispossessed, confused—
    Fugitive footprints
     with destinies unread—unlived
      soon to be liquefied, eclipsed
       by currents that transcend self

With each tide's face
 a different ephemeral tree of life
  is ingranuled
   A unique map
    palm of hand, veined in sand
     Beginning, erasing, beginning, erasing
      again and again

The lyrical waters
 in their continuity of change
  refurbish, purify
   nursing any rawness

(continued)

The boundless energies of the sea
  generously transmute electricities, energies
    into and down
      my inner rivers, streams

I am receptive
  surrendering resistance
    as if to a loved one
      allowing him
        allowing the sea
          to encompass me
          A soothing lullaby
            in the fusion
              of our rhythms

When the day turns its back
  losing sight of nocturnal mysteries
    Skies, sands, sea color one
      Rocks absorb the blackness
        of a future midnight

I see this amniotic world
  of the primordial
    flash back centuries
      returning to this moment
        in a moment
          The beginning, beginnings
            the first gurgle
              is heard
                as it was
                  so long ago
                    before all

I sense, feel
  the untamed orchestration
    of the eternal
      An elating peace, relief
        as I breathe
          infused in the infinite

silence answers us
in our mirrored lake of compose

Pyramid

My hungry thirst
is quenched by primal seas
infusing my veins
I bathe in endless oceans
that birth all things
that are also—me

These golden juices
flower honey throughout my being
Hummingbirds whirr
from my every edge
My spirit so pollinated
takes flight
beyond me

This polarity
born of my blossomed flower
absorbs life's golden nectar
from within

The beams of my centered star
  reach into timelessness

The abundant moment of me
  fills the universe

My rays fuse
  with celestial beings

Flight feathers my arms
  soaring me beyond origin

Countless leaves of me
  fly into breezes

Never to land
  only transform

As the skies countenance
ever changes
Nomadic sands
ever drift
          So it is

My path thus sublimely lit
  crystal clear in purity, purpose

I breathe expanded
  in the open temple of myself

The ultimate of knowing
                    the eternal

III

Chapter of Visionaries

"madness" alone, can save
give the spirit its revolution

there is no life
in the acceptance of the dark shade of limited thought

Survival Through Illumination

Black seas boil
      bursting questions
            toward the heavens
Rejected
      they drop
           unanswered
             outraged
These turbulent waves
        crash their despised selves
           into a kaleidoscope
             of meaningless mobile fragments
Dirty sick froth
      bubbling with dead hate
           lays licking
             sandless shores

Curdling
    as
      evil has conquered

Overwhelming death scents
toxify my air
weak
I am sucked into
whirlpools
of
magnetic unknowns

Drowning
I lose consciousness
disintegrate
into
quiet aqua waters
below

Isolated
I shake with the cold of paralysis
awaiting

the thaw of illumination

the imprisoning bars of society
are made
of the self-hate of guilt's archaic traditions

No to Guilt

Allow the buried to die
     Stay there
Do not hear their screams
     Nor water their graves with your tears
Tears that must be stopped
     Before they crystallize into bitter icycles
Daggers that boomerang, Plunge
     piercing within

Stomp on the ground
     Do not allow any holes for their breathing
Do not permit their predacious octopi arms
     to suck you into their mire of entrails
Letting them feign care for you
     in their leukemic embrace

I am trudging through the pages of the Bible
    the dried blood of its scroll
                sticks to my soles
My body stretched
          across the rack of world suffering
I am striking, holding revolutions
        fighting life—death
             wars of the centuries
I feel the bleeding
        watch it flood the rivers
            the pain sobs in my blood
I eat the ashes of the dead
        vomit my hatred
            of their bitter taste
They breathe their agony into me
        while
        I am powerless to resuscitate them
Furiously
    I tear into their scars
        attempting to heal
           only revealing
             grinning toothless mouths

After awhile
    Anguish, avenged
        separates its life from mine
    Its voice for now
        quiescent within me

Greed

her flower is ravaged
by
the mildew of greed

the center ravished
tasting rot
as
the roots thirst

parasites eagerly weave
their webby trap
from leaf to flower
encapturing her

their woven net
transports, escalates
them to devour
finally swallow their source

he was like
a grain of rice
that had never been cooked
awakened or expanded

he was rigid as a nail
unreceptive to any 'would'

don't peck into me
as a woodpecker on a tree
using my back to aid in mutilating me

Hate
a
volcanic boil
aches
to be released
this self-concocted poison
paralizes   nullifies
as it
whirlpools
within
erupting
into
boiling lava
burning destruction
indiscriminately

I wonder if in fighting the disease of death
you become stronger
as if you've had a vaccination
and after having a bout and surviving,
achieve a freedom in your living

I also think it's like an allergy—
if you're over-exposed
you over-react
to that which you're vulnerable
and are weakened
unless suitable defenses are adapted

silence can be pregnant with nutritious solitude
or
heavy with malignant toxics

neither have sound
but
opposite electricities
inhabit
them

Invisible Evils

Nocturnal wings
of colossal widths, encircle—ensnare
with nets of ominous cloaked shadows

Captives are sought—selected
those ripened, prone to self-sacrifice
innocent to forthcoming toxic infusions

Claws, beak, all weapons
are veniferously dipped
to sap, suck, drain
These vulturine creatures
transfuse their dryness
with the nectar of the succulent

Silently raping all assailable atmospheres
Distilling the mobile, leaving lichens
Bleaking meadows, gardens into opaque deserts
Vaporizing effervescence, buoyancy into obscure disintegration

Human bombs of spiritual demolition
shrouded in mystic archaism

Roots knot, choking in their epidemic of unawareness
Submarines of evil creep
unrecognized, except by those who trust their senses
unperceived by recoiled antennae

(continued)

Unstylized pirates
with eyebrows of bats in flight
Mouths swooping in looping nooses
Teeth chomping with sounds of no roots
rob, mesmerize, cajole incessantly

Even in their ghost-like sleep
the air is gleaned into dehydration
These chameleons of hypocrisy blend
disguised into atmospheres

Cloaked shadows
predatorily loom, lurk, net again
Emitting acrid odors
when their vestibules wither dry

Sacrifices are demanded—hunted
to placate, resuscitate the veniferous abyssmal thirst

Their stone cold kiss coagulates

Multiple surrenders of life
feed the process of metempsychosis
necessary to the existence of
these creatures of ashy paleness
Those who died so many centuries ago

Twitching now
with the seeping warmth of fresh essence
transfused from another
who now will be the convalescent of
a spiritual anemia and bodily leukemia

Probably questioning their feeling of weakness

when you speak to my soul
my cup of self is filled
when my soul is not touched
my cup feels dry

they were looking in their own mirrors
too small for each other's face

when the essence
from the marrow of my being
is felt by another
I am fortified

the "am" of my core
is being lived, known—
fantasized dependencies vanish

when I am mis-felt   mis-understood
put out of focus
through another's lack of,
or different evolvement of growth
it is a dry experience

when I am related to
through another's projection, fantasy, or need
my soul is left solitary
false dependencies are ignited
the people who relate to me the least
I may feel I need the most
because the "am" of me
has been temporarily fragmented
by this mis-connection

Fire as . . .

Red passion
    the spirit's blood fuel
        erupts, enflames
            validating the pulse of warriors
                in revolt, strikes, all transitions

A suffering—purification
    The alchemy of renewal

This sulphur defies stagnation
    demands innovation

But fire consumes
    its flames devour

A new passage must be spun
    just as the spider spins a ladder
        to escape capture

Survival instincts are unrelenting spurs
    offering no choice, involuntary
        if life is to go on . . .

seclusion insists on my presence
for my spiritual survival

Solitude is Whole

My own arms encircle me
I am whole again
as much as I love to love

I need to sleep inside first

one of the consistent alchemies of life
is its contradictions

Electricities are linear kinetic energies
        that recharge each other from their explosions . . .
            Opposites are imperative
                for this reforming
                    of energy patterns
                        Needing to decompose
                            for death to give birth

    Gave thought to

                        Masochism or self-destructive tendencies
                    could be thresholds—
                inciters to the opposite of self-destruction
            by destroying one pattern of behavior
        and redesigning it into another

                        This process is imperative for creativity

Eternal Self

I think of death now
as a pregnant dynamic
I fear less the endings
as to be living in finites
is to be living in the infinite

I fear less
the loss of myself—others
as I know, not only sense
our energies speak, breathe, ride
infused in the currential waves of space
echoing our timeless densities
from our destinies

I left a candle burning by my bed
my spirit wasn't ready to be alone
the candle would keep it company
though the rest of me was tired
my spirit burned on—needing more
into the night
Unlike the candle
my spirit will never burn out
even when the rest of me demands sleep

Primal Desire

My breasts swell
I am impregnated with the primal desire
to birth you
your feelings
To encourage your emergence
into the coldness
that once so shocked you
as
to freeze your soul

I try again
to exceed your natural mother
to be your lover
to impregnate you with my pulse, passion
transfuse your heart to breathe

As in the total surrender of birth
I liquefy my being
into the blood of my passion
for your deliverance
Only that power might free you
to feel

(continued)

You hate me
rejecting your spirit's birth
denying your hate
for the one
who pushed you from her wound
not from her life

Thus born a wound
you've never loved

I am different from her
will you ever know?
will I?

Your hurt is of the deepest
as it was born in your origination

Only in this mutual depth of pain
can we meet
possibly heal
be re-born through each other

Now
I know the answer
the agony
the wrestling to understand
the conscious tearing to comprehend
such pain
subsides

No longer
distort
label this passion neurosis
but
declare the miracle
of the
ravaging creative instinct
to heal

IV

Chapter of Musings

fantasies are symphonies
our hearts play to our souls

Hibernation

I want to be
a brown heavily furred earth animal
burrow deep into rich soil
deep in a cave
with books, paper, and pen
enough rays of the sun's hair
for warmth and light
flowers to sprout fragrance
vegetables to nourish
a return totally to a beginning
of unfiltered, untaught, untouched
Life

The Moon's Placenta

I bathe in the glow
    of the moon's blue silver
it envelopes me in silence
      serene whispers urge
         my inward streams to
           move deeper
             further
                 ever further
back into
  the ageless centuries of beginnings
  I slide down a wondrous waterfall
           of these mercurial moments
Landing in
      the lucid pool of the present

I would choose
if
I had a wish to be
No   not be you
be me
But borrow your wings
Boundless and free   Universally be
a Gypsy Bird of the Sea
Not to think how it feels
but feel what it is
Flying with flocking feathers following me
White bird-face cast sunly

Freedom's breath inhaling me
a
Gypsy bird gliding
spheres of symphony

Elation

I walk alone above the earth
  elevated by the erotic jasmine of freedom

Sun-ray fingers comb my hair
  transmitting sparks of flaming gold

My eyes are variegated leaves inter-dancing

All that grows breathes through me
  I spring from this force streaming out
    as it cascades into musical ribbons

Full Moon in Hydra, Greece

the moon's magic swallows
  the hilly port of Hydra
    her remote silence
      enshrouds white washed walls
        with haunting secrets
                her elusive face illuminates
              each cobblestone passageway
            her mercurial shadows
            breathe paths of mystic promise

Candied Fields

the children
  petals and stems
    all colors, all sizes

a rollicking meadow
  of lollipop flowers

flavor the breezes
  lemon and orange

I am a laughing gypsy
flying the piney sea
this tall forest of pointed trees
spurs me up
upon stars for feet
I'm close enough
to touch the moon
embracing her cool round
knowing, for now
I'm no longer
part of that
below

ground

Things

a Thing is only what we see
what we see through ourselves
therefore it is only a Thing
unless we feel it otherwise

we must become part of a Thing
for it to mean anyThing
otherwise it is the world's possession
                    impersonalized

so why acquire before we feel
what we want to be part of us
it becomes an extra tooth
                or someThing otherwise

Collage of Malibu Pier

It's a beginning that ends—
An end that begins
A bridge that stops unlike other paths—
its wooden back refuses most designs of travel

An indented paragraph over waters
With an exclamation point to the sky

A wedding held in cool colors
uniting the familiar with the unknown

A carnival of odors saltily moistened

A bouillabaise of faces above and below

Conversations tossed, not captives of purpose

Insensitive radios interrupt the voices of nature

Spontaneity currented by the transitory

The infinite of life prospers
in a vast sea of questions—hooking answers
that may bite, be caught, or swim on

when I give my opinions, passions, creations
whatever energy I project
reflects the evolvement, climate of my interior

Synvision

The eyes are the lens of the mind
brain tissue looking out
nearsightedness
and
farsightedness
are indicators
of the mind's relationship
with the world

Unshared

degraded in dusty spider laces
    faded books hide unshared faces
hearts imprinted on unread pages
    die, waiting on shelves for ages

I want to be a gypsy bird
                    tipping tops of pines

Following my instincts
                    and fragrances of skies

Gusty waves of cosmic tides
                    sweep my wings
                              above their flight

I am a bird in its most ultimate delight

holidays, rituals, enforced celebrations of all kinds
are like balloons being blown up
by the hot air of their psychological dynamics—
this amplification of their reality
offers truth if we desire awareness

New Year's Eve

My heart is free'd
>>as confetti tossed
>>>>on New Year's Eve

My head
>>flooded with multicolors
>>>>swirls, spinning me
>>>>>into wild ribbons
>>>>>>of laughing hats

Balloons
>>burst me into abandon
>>>>off into skies

I ride on
>>winds of feathered air

The lunar's mercury
>>beckons me this night
>My heart
>>>>races to every furthest corner
>>>>>touching places
>>>>>>never felt before

>Fickle, fragile
>>>>streamers of itself
>>>>>are left
>>>>>>everywhere

V

Chapter of Visages

as the birds instinctively migrate at a certain time of year
so my life is led

Beyond Choice

My soul adventures
   not hearing me
      it has an autonomous life
         needing—demanding
           mobility   air   nourishment
              intellectually, physically
                sensually, instinctually
                  requiring expansion
                      and song

her beauty is part of her being
she does not wear it
as her personal accomplishment

Quintessence

I want to lie under a shadowy tree
  with many dark green glossy leaves
    with deep foresty scents, musky scents
      of recent rains, dampening, clinging
        wetting my lips, moistening me
          to embrace my tree, my man, my lover
            whose shadows include all of me
              not leaving an edge out

I want to rest there, beneath him
  and share from me, my fragrance—
    petals—self—cover him
      cover more than his shadow

Rainbow his being with my colors
  so he will never be quite the same again
    just that much closer to heaven
      for having felt my beauty

the over-stuffed child, my ex-lover
relates to me now as his legendary mother

daughter, sister, lover
face, body, and a mother
related to as the Need
of another

Defining

In knowing you, your sympathies, essence
  the blend of juices that flow
    forming you as you go
      in knowing you in these depths
        I understand myself better

In resistance to another's identity
  I define myself more clearly
    our stems which grow so differently
      bear such different leaves and fruits

His Needs

The night wore layers of clothes, unpeeled
Heavy shawls of silence enshrouded the walls
The windows and doors kept mouths tightly sealed

I must get away before he calls—
his footsteps would be faint
The seas outside muffle my hearing
now fear in crawls

He lies on the floor with arms to confide
His eyes dancing with stolen stars from the skies
He wound himself to me; Fiercely implied:

> you are mine to serve me, my needs not told
> you are mine to worship under my knee
> embrace me child love, don't be cold

Soft and yielding I looked up with no plea
His crashing self swallowing me, caught fire
He gripped through to my bones:

> you'll do and I'll be
> your destiny is me, and my desire
> is for sweet you to serve my needs, Don't tire

She Was Widowed First

She became your wife and your widow
Widowed, when she married her spirit
to your lack of one
In the first contagious breath
you breathed through her

She was a pollinator of life
A defier of death
when she challenged you   Satan on

Then, later
    She demanded revenge for your rape of her light
    Riding a wild beast
    she used this four-legged vehicle for escape
    Falling to the ground to an early death

Thus
    She had unbridled herself at last
    in this accident claiming a freedom
    Her body was sacrificed
    She unsaddled you from her back

But
    You kept her grave open
    her coffin unclosed within you
    Your dry veins thirsted
    You continued to scavenge, ravish her

Since
    Your dungeon was dank, dark, airless
    Her pilot light was snuffed out
    by your rasping breath

Hence, involuntarily
    You freed her for her final retaliation
    Releasing her to close her own coffin
                cover her own grave

Behind your black opaque eyes
that can't reflect
the light of any sun

You feel betrayed
        Your robbery was pocketless

Vampire

his lips were thin and tight
his eyes were agates of night
his mane hung black and loose
he was hardened to jungle's blight
his neck stooped, through his self-made noose
false laughter hid his buried plight
while he thirsted for love's warm juice

The Father—a Thief of Life

he seeks the life
he doesn't have
living through his sons

burning their youth out
balding their young minds

burdening their unformed spines
with the immobilizing anchor
                of
                his
        abyssmal void

Their Father—the Fisherman

his daughters were drugged and seduced
by the intimidation of heavy lines
he hung them with money hooks
money bait was tantalizing
he knew they'd always bite
from the end of heavy lines
he teased with lover's words

their passion's hunger
loved him with hate

words cost nothing
bait was cheap
seduction masked death's hook

fear chose ignorance for eyes
their eyes dim and glassy
reflected their man above
his pole bent in half
with the weight of his catch

usually a person's strongest capacity
parents their weakest

His Life is a Eulogy

Outside
A withered hull of corn
Inside
A yellow tooth-less cob
           Eaten up.
           You are gone
Sacrificed to dreams of immortality
           Performing
as your own tyrannical puppet
           Creating memorial upon memorial
           Demanding that you would never die
           You never lived

Now you'll die twice

The Thornless Rose

she stands
nude   vulnerable   threatened
only a few glossy leaves on her wavering slim stem

holding her loved ones with velvet petaled palms
she gives the pink love
her gentleness never knew
maybe this would bring the love
this soft one never had
but, as her scent is given and lost
her leaves brown and brittle

The young ones grow larger, stronger, angrier
They demand all—more
All—More
her flower is eaten by the mildew of greed

the last petal drops
is stepped on
left crushed, unnoticed
her unprotected core is exposed
the thorns never grew

The strong angry ones yell
More—More
You're depriving us

the rose strains to regrow her petals
but
her velvet palm is shorn

she has withered from her roots

she lays down like a human floormat
for others to wipe their feet
then discreetly cleans away their dirty tracks

you might as well lie down on a buffet table
for the emotional cannibals to help themselves
all they leave are the discarded crumbs of you

Empty

She loved so much
in a mad sort of way
that she lost herself
in her man claimed as prey

Facial skin sucked in
haunted and tight
led a body around
emptied and light

She attempted to
crawl inside of him
loosing her soul
pulsing only through him

Vacancy echoed
her tortured wail
all that remained
was illusion's betrayal

Selves Dissolved

Our fruits bled
     from the hypnotic vine of myth
This deep ripened burgundy
     flowed, ebbed
        Once swallowed,
          consumed us
    in the aphrodisiac of surrender

You are a hurricane
You are the wind of my life
making me breathless
Blowing my hair here—there
not staying anywhere of me
long enough to know me
really know me
You move so fast in your currents
Excitement to touch—feel—
in seconds spread my pollen, honey
all over you
into your eager mouths
My currents blend into yours
our rhythms excite me
I am blown away from myself
out of control—lost within yours
ah—

I feel like pollen . . .

winds, breezes send the pollen of me everywhere
I don't know where it lights
where it sprouts
who is touched with greenness
I want to see
the climates of my pollen reflected
in your eyes
your touch
your warmth heating my blossoms
feel the sun of my love for you
in you—be warmed by it
for it to thaw your long winters
your tears not to be so cold

bridled by the reins of heredity
held by parents of different blood
orphaned by no mutuality—
saddled by the tight girth of unrequited needs

oh pathetic clown with the face of your audience
you're playing with others' lives
not having your own to live

The Void is Larger

In the deepest caverns of the darkest part of you
Orphaned winds wail
of your longing hungers
Echoing raw agony everywhere
In the dim flatness of your brown eyes
In the escalating roles of flesh
you wrap around and round
Insulating yourself from your world of looming threats
In your hollow caverns
lies an embryo thrashing—
impotent screams, demands
Desperately trying to fool yourself and others
not to see through
the powerful appearing man
tossing his boyish charm with abandon
disguising yet sensing
the void
within
is larger than
himself

essence is the juice of the spirit
generating, re-creating life

Please Heal

I shape the blood velvet
           of rose petals
upon your dry dim eyes
Eyes shut with hurt

Your tears deserve a fragrance

The petals darken, drop
absorbed with your bruises,
gift your eyes
with their dew

Our pupils collide
Their black disks fuse
           swirling us
into one infinite tunnel

We see the blood
of our rose stains
           beneath us

Our spirits
     re-scented
         taste of glorious moistures

You Live in the Past

burning rays
leave your body's sun
heating me
alchemizing the climate of us

I need to evolve—transform
dance in the heated circle of our light
but
your powerful rays
burn you
inducing sleep . . .

you slumber
with
pillows of yesterdays
over your head

pillow cases
of
memories
suffocate
our
todays

what we share
cannot be defined
it transcends the conceptions born of the terrestial—
singing eternally as part of the infinite

Child of Truth

I want a child
born of our blossom

A birth of all
    we have been
        can be

Our fusion
caught in time
by an explosion
    of our fire

Another first world
    created by us
with the passion
    of ourselves
    for our
chosen God's Life

Formed in truth
our immortal child
whose music is
our dance of life

cliffs of experience
  have step-less ladders
  offering the jolts necessary
  for sunlit returns

Experience . . .

We spread our wings
Dared speak with the sun

You flew too close
Melting away

I took a shocking fall
The sun's heat missed me for days

I changed my earth
but you stayed
stuck to the sun's wounding rays
Consumed by them

unchanged

I miss the scent of your madness
Your dim drowned eyes
I would fling myself
into

We would swim together
Splashing in the currents of our streams
Basking along shores
Living the unlimited

I miss you beloved one
though our passions
sank us

Withdrawal

Needs too great
but all enchained
enclosed in one's own womb
no better than self-burial
in a tomb

Fresh air
chains broken loose
stark nude
more frightening
than lewd

to be a prisoner within oneself
closed as it may feel
less with the world
one must deal

it's easier to act out the myth of me
than to be what I am
I've had so little practice being me
except alone

I suffer from the dis-ease of not being understood

Loneliness

How would the earth feel without roots of plants

　　　　　　Plants without earth

Love without youth

　　　　　　Youth without love

Birds without wings

　　　　　　Wings without birds

To have a strong voice

　　　　　　Seldom answered beyond its own echo

Gypsy Youth of the Sea

deep
royal
electric
eyes of the sea
I want to see them again
because of their depth of blue
are they a mere reflection
or more
as the skies beyond

the
scent
of
sea-salt
mixed
with the heat
of your sun-goldened skin
I want to taste our moistures again

your
body
warm
but
cool
your leanness so yielding

the
heavy tangled texture
of your
wind-whipped mane
like toasted sands
after
wind storms
I want my fingers caught in its midst again

(continued)

you feel
born
of the seas   skies   suns
the
mounded sand dunes
of time
your home

no beginnings
endings
your current moves
with
the rhythm of incessant tides

This Man is His Trees

High buxom hills
  golden rolling mounds
    these soft yielding mistresses
      your flaxen hay'd mistresses
        offer their ripened grains
          to the birthing green of your eyes
            Your eyes that possess them
              meadow their silkened lashes
                flirting waving tresses
                  mingled with ribboned petals

Their cleavage homes your trees
  The tall tree of you
    branches shade for your women—
      your sunned earth-mounds
        guarding them from scorch or dry

This family of you
  rooted deep
    within your fertile passion
    shares your breath

Faith in my Daughters

A struggle to watch—
feel my loved child suffer
Her antennae smashed

I yearn to shield her paleness
It isn't possible to protect her
        from what she is not

With faith
I see her grow
   into more of what she is
             living herself
               instead of through me

Soul Daughter

I looked into
those enormous blue mirrors
of black fringed life
they went around and round

Her blue pools of eternities
lured me
drawing me into
her soul ethereal

Our pupils matched each others
she said
I love you
you will live forever
because
you are love

My tears knew
all of me knew

I am blessed with a
daughter of my soul

A Living Poem

I feel inadequate
  at attempting to put into words
    paint, photograph
      or in any way recreate
        the unique quality of my young child
          lying on the couch
            her Boticelli rose face
              leafed by brown earth hues—
                lustrous hair shining of life
                lashes crescently shaped
                rest on her slumber

Her fertile beauty speaks
  of the depth of her spiritual love
    breathing, pervading
      through her clasped hands on my knee
        her face upturned in total belonging

Love flooded through me
  as I wept silently
    the tears wetting my hair
      in the most
        delicate of strong feelings

She was a poem herself
  impossible to recreate
    but impossible not to try to
      Her passion of being
        was to be luxuriously felt

Words refuse to be of any consequential help

The most genuine poem is breathing, on my knee

Unnamed Source

My back shapes an earthen bed
I yearn upwards
My eyes ride along silvery beams, meeting planets
I am a planet myself
round, sparkling, flowing
fusing yet mercurial
My roots go far beyond self
beyond corners, boundaries
They reach, dig, branch, seed, blossom into territories
I sense but haven't seen, yet know
My roots drink from undiscovered or forgotten wells
I am part of more than I can know
I enjoy not knowing
Discoveries are constant
I am part of all that has been
is, will be
A plant, a tree of a person
My spirit soars from its source instinctively
as a wolf howls to the full moon
I am akin to the bowels of life
Its pulse races through my streams
My spirit is juicy
Its roots stand thick
in the fertile waters of where the world was born
Ah—I feel it so

VI

Chapter of Spleen

we are taught first
to eyelessly look up to images and symbols
instead of looking first into the eyes of ourselves

the need for defense
is far greater than the need to expand
thus society protects what is not
rather than what is—
as few reach beyond defense

Alienation

My eyes ache
  with the weight of keeping
    the cataclysmic split of myself together
      in one body, one land

I am split
  between my visions and what my eyes see
    unable to live in a land
      analogous to my enlightenment

making life static
embalms it

The Robot

man's in a trance
a slow death dance
    he's just
an inorganic tool
      covering
concrete guts to duel
      computerized
unlived lives
    in
self-made sterile hives
      gulping
instant numbered flab food
spit for the dummy's tube
      ebbing
blood drips each day
anesthesized away
     a zoo
of numb civilization
     with no
spiritual realization
     the robot
man's in a trance
a slow death dance

what I know
is my saddle to ride the wild horse of life
sometimes I ride bareback
my questions give me spurs toward undefined paths
a bridle would limit both

marrowless teachings
grow skeletal prisons

an answer's greatest contribution
is to incite you to other questions

spiders do not need to go to school
to be
intricately fine architects

a supreme reason to question
the basis of civilization's schooling
which methodically structures—destructively

causing you to unlearn
that which is innately within
then you learn it superficially
losing your origin of learning

educere—Latin for education—means
"to bring out that which is within"

Doctors Appt.

Driving
lower
lower
into
anemic air
unseen by attendants
with
non-reflecting eyes
directed by automatic hands
signaling to a much valued
thing
Called
a Parking Space

Entombed
in this
cement catacomb
wailing
of
modern man's ills
this hole below
Called
Subterranean Parking

Leads
you up again
on futile wheels
up onto
suffocated earth
Called
a Driveway

(continued)

Returning
to a
hole above
Called
Civilization

Where
grey punished faces
cough grey sick air
entering
sun-less tombs
built from
soul-less concepts
Called
Highrise Buildings

Designed
for
greedy doctor factories
leasing icy cells
charging
people to see
if they are still
alive
and if so
What to do
About
It

how I wonder about a sense of values
when I see someone showing off his house of impeccable taste
where all the dead things are being cared for
and all the live things are dying

you must be bigger
than what you are creating
otherwise
you become Its object

Buildings Downtown

Those dominating buildings downtown
vault the light hours
of the somnabulist dead

Our meteoric times
offer burial before death
in these reincarnations of Egyptian tombs

Unwrapped mummies and daddies drift;
alibis, self-enshrouded
Auto pilots set—
their opaque gaze
matches the lidless stare
of elevator buttons . . .

These spaced out phantoms float
embalmed in leukemic air
Recording a zero pulse
Cemented in blocked circulation

A malignant silence hovers
Congestion rules

Mankind's juices leak
into the desert cactus of greed and power

Big profits reek of the
Excrement of the Dead

greed parents poverty

Tahiti and Other Places

The natives no longer hold hands
embracing stems with nature

Only the lush brown velvet of their skins
still matches their earth
Under, churns the mechanics of anxiety
the emotional industry of materialization

The earth in its technicolor fecundity
hollers of sublime abundance
                    with its
honeyed perfumes, sunburst mangoes, milky rich coconuts

Every leaf offers its juice of life

All become impotent sacrifices

The native stands alienated
Famine of spirit is not fed
by fish-rich seas
or the heaviness of trees

In clenching his fist
Sensing tyranny's oppressive net
He exchanges his captive's freedom
for self-enslavement

Now, sterilized
he is akin to the inert volcanoes
their hollowness echoing him

Nature is raucous
Victorious in Be-ing
Mindless

But, in the brain of man
lay the atoms of destruction

No bombs are needed

usually the reason
a person so-called succeeds in society's structure
is the same reason he fails as a human
in order to succeed within society's work slots
you first must be de-humanized

your be-ing must be developed
first
in order to define
your ultimate meaning;
it is not your do-ing
that in itself
can give your be-ing
its essential meaning

existing according to society's values
one is recognized as sane
therefore is in-sane—
to live rather than exist
is to dare to be out-sane

no beehive
for me
loosing myself
in its
cells
an automaton
programmed
to buzz
for unchosen honey

leaving myself a hollow hive

he was like a chameleon
unrecognizable even unto himself

No Identity

the earth
   inhabited by puppets impersonating
      their strings
         worn to feeble threads
            defeated grasps
               to connect with origin
                  puppets
                    no face
                       no strings
                                 an Exit from life

Kashmir, India

Meadows of singing trees
  fling open arms
    Arms studded with yellow jewels
     Jewels that blossom ripe fruit
      seeking to feed, comfort the poor

Pink budded trees
  bouffant as ballerinas
   sway in fragile grace
   asking no money
    for their gifts of joy

These pastel choruses
  serenade the poor
   as they slave
    further into the ground
     Unholy in their holes
      Filth cornered in bleak monotones

Breezes moan low
        to the wretched curled feet of man

Moonstone lakes of serene face
  hum silent prayers
   Their calmness reflects
    the troups of trees
     composing God's portraits

Their soft hymns
  herald the dark slave
   Nature seeks to care for

accepting society's values
would be like checking into the nearest morgue on foot

cities are incubators
of people breathing through each other's lungs

a symbol of civilization's self-destruction
is an ambulance unable to get through the traffic

the American adult feeds the youth fad
with his atrophy of spirit
only able to degenerate into an impersonation of life
not demanding to live the dignity
that may be born
of his own intrinsic wisdom

Splat

Life versus Death
  the City offers Lobotomies
    a Sensation-jammed diet
     of no substance
       Narcotics to pinprick the dead
         Pinprick through emotional anesthesia

a fading, de-synthesized
  hostile, valium-soaked tribe
   of dead-to-dying performers

Performers at everything
  doing nothing
   in nothing
    nothing within

People as bleached white bread
  de-vitaminized
    Enslaved by no passions—void
     the inability to seek, know
      another human's being

Plagiarizing truth
  frenetic, hysterical

Epileptic Disassociation
  in every form

(continued)

Sensation in grotesque fluorescence
  A bleaking of fertility, sperm, egg,
    earth, ocean, skies

All leukemic, bleached, blanched lichens
  mechanical twitches, switches, defenses
    reactions—Living Spasms

Movements crippled by coagulating circulations
  Skulls so tight
    furrows so deep
      Vestibules stuffed with newspapers
        Devoid of seed, self, core

The transformation of blood into numbers
  Money, the giant green and black scapegoat
    made from black ashes
      The Remains of life-fires burned out
        A contagious Alibi for the
          Plague of the Spirit

The startling Awareness of
  the inorganic—inanimate
    Triumphant over too many

insensitivity feeds false power, greed, manipulation
what is sought outside
is to compensate for the lack inside
if power is intrinsic
to capture it outside is unneeded

like a grey death pallor
the pallor of no faith
can erase truth
the truth that is the red food of life

Circles of Death

I have been fighting death
  all my life
    in the paralysis of greed and power
      in the poisons of those
        who have never lived life

                I see fears
                  scarring vision, blinding men
                  ensnaring them into herds
                of dazed anonymous slaves

I see a giant zero
  entombing the universe
    as it rotates slowly

    A dying disk recording,
      whining of its abuse
        at being played at the wrong speed, volume
          through alien speakers

        I am encircled by civilization's zero
          pained by the noose of its passivities—
        faces strain, trying for nothingness
          with the panic
        of their secret knowing of the zero

The never beginning, never ending zero
  Circles   Wheels
    Circles   Wheels
      Circles   Wheels
          Around and Around

                    Until time pronounces it is time
                      to drop from the outside circle
                      the futile wheel of zero
                      into the middle, the Earth

To sterilize the soil
  for the still born
    who will then rejoin
      the outside circle

the quality of God we seek outside
is analogous to our God within

his unrelenting intuitive winds
tunnel mountains
with the propulsion of his truths

the soil determines the blossom of its seed
man must seek that soil which can flower his soul

the more we believe in ourselves
the less we need to see to believe—
we see through ourselves
therefore we all see differently, need differently
with enough belief, remain unique

Circles of Life

Only a few
with the miracle of spirit
keep alive
This glorious universal seed
implanted within
has more verve, is vaster than
the zero world outside

When they fall
into the middle, the earth
they have fed the circle
they have pollinated all
they touch
They flower meadows
wherever there is life
but sadly
they see burnt arrid lands
unreceptive to birth
scorched with the dryness
of dead spirit

These few
struggle to protect their miracle
usually unrecognized by others
but
sought and abused

They are drained
as
the few fresh water springs
available
in
times of vast spiritual drought

Semantic Aphasia

Words Words Words
Why is it so necessary to
use these linear spiritless formations
to attempt communication
Speech is crimed in subterfuge, manipulation,
games to avoid contact
A verbal Halloween overcelebrated

Language is so often more relevant in its absence—
when a person's essence unfurls from him
it silently vocalizes his own atmosphere
in unique electricities, colors, textures
that unfurl from him

(continued on page 233)

the artist of sound re-creates nature's voice

Nature's speech is innocent, continuously virginal
Artless in her art
Her language is in being, has flesh
breathes undiffused from her center of truth
Nature does not ingratiate—
without hesitation can be trusted, embraced

Nature's sacred hymns are heard murmuring
in lush growth fructifying, in creatures banqueting

The morning's balm is mellifluous
in its placenta of renewal
The heavy rich soul of earth blushes deeper brown
sighing with the swells of its massive deliveries

The outrageous Himalayas
coating blue white radiance
shout of their frozen freedom in electrifying silence
These unrestrainable mountainous heroes
fling laughter boldly
echoing their impact beyond all spheres

The spoken word awaits response
Nature's voice awaits none—
requesting no validation for her being
She is salubrious, rejuvenating

Winds, lightning, storms, droughts all have a language
whose dynamic matches our human evolutions, climates within
But when nature is strangulated,
leukemized in man's immobilities of concrete, steel,
toxified in illness of industry—
her death sirens are heard only by those who can interpret her muteness

(continued on page 235)

233

people think in terms of words
not using the integration of their senses
to speak or listen

Quality of speech
relates to the quality of evolvement of person

Words are empty receptacles
encasements open-mouthed,
waiting to be filled—
transfused from spiritless matter into
cathedrals, swords, blossoms, or tombs
depending on what we feed them
Fleshless skeletons
before they've been metabolized by us
To be organic, words must be lived—
eaten, digested, grow bodies, breathe through us

Relevant, genuine, artistic communication is so precious
Instead, words are swung as weapons
The difference between truth and lie must be amplified
to exemplify the differentiation

(continued on page 237)

ears are antennae—receivers
picking up currents, waves, electricities—
the comprehension of your mind
determines how many channels are available
for you to tune in to

Words are like the combustion from machines
waters from a spring, vitamins from food
The derivative can only have the life of its source
Inane talk is futile, unfertile
just dust, amounting to nothing—coming from nowhere

Platitudes, ambiguities,
all ritualistic verbalization is an indignity
Mechanized static from human tape decks
A desert of bleached voices coming from those whose pilot light is out
Prattle hammering at you, not to you
Oral jogging, leaving you flabby, desensitized from the abuse

Verbal building blocks
piling formations
on which you are sitting
on the top of articulated garbage
Either you leap off
and it topples over
or you keep piling
hoping to find the meaning eventually

Ideal semantics is a sharing of blood
A phone not needing a cord
A symbolic chanting from the primal seas of being
A flow of exchange of one's nectar, fruits
In camaraderie, love, conflict
this fusing is a nourishing feast
A burial of isolation

(*continued on page 239*)

Poetry of the senses
is unformulable, solitary—
For words to live
this transcendence of exalted passion
they must breathe first
in the pulse of their parent

Whoever breathes God—body—flesh
can metabolize the inanimate, the word
is in that transfusion
a deity among the deities

writing revives my dignity